THE BATSFORD COLOUR BOOK OF

Norfolk

Introduction and commentaries by
Philip Hepworth

B. T. BATSFORD LTD   LONDON

First published 1976

Filmset by
Servis Filmsetting Ltd, Manchester
Printed and bound by
Lee Fung Asco, Hong Kong
for the publishers B. T. Batsford Ltd,
4 Fitzhardinge Street, London W1H 0AH

ISBN 0 7134 3154 7

Contents

Acknowledgments

The Publishers would like to thank the following for permission to reproduce the colour transparencies in this book:

A. P. Cooper, pages 29, 37, 39;
Noel Habgood, pages 23, 25, 27, 35, 47, 53, 59;
A. F. Kersting, pages 21, 49, 55, 61, 63;
Picturepoint Ltd, pages 31, 33, 43, 45;
Kenneth Scowen, pages 17, 19, 51, 57;
Spectrum, page 41.

Introduction

If Norfolk differs from other counties, it does so in being considered remote, despite the popularity of the Broads, the Golden Mile at Yarmouth and the well-attended coastal resorts of Cromer and Sheringham. The Queen has a country home at Sandringham, near one of the county's larger resorts, Hunstanton, and its capital city Norwich is finely and centrally situated, unlike some other county towns. Being much larger than Great Yarmouth, the next town in size, Norwich is unquestionably in the lead, the seat of the Crown Courts, of the county government and of its own district government. Its charm lies in its variety and breadth of interest. Some two hours by rail from London, it embraces the largest insurance company outside London, and the largest number of mediaeval churches not excepting London.

Although Norwich has suffered mistakes in post-war rebuilding they cannot measure up to its triumphs. Take first the river Wensum which divides the city unequally between North and South, though so effectively that the builders of Norwich's mediaeval walls left off when they arrived at the river. In recent years the City Council, aided by voluntary bodies and owners, has laid out paths and seats making it possible for the first time for the public to walk and settle down alongside the river banks. At the central yacht station of what was looked on as the port of Norwich one may journey by passenger boat to Coldham Hall, a few miles downstream. Previously it was not often possible to see the river in passing except in its upper reaches, even Riverside Road being blanked off by hoardings. As its contribution to European Architectural Heritage Year Norwich City Council and associated groups have opened up the central riverside and built houses facing the river banks at Friars' Quay, an historic central crossing point.

Over-the-Water, the northern district of small workers' houses which has been tidied up by this restoration scheme, is a most historic part of the city containing many buildings which are now more accessible.

St George's Church houses the tomb of John Crome, founder of the Norwich School of Painting; St Michael's at Coslany has most lavish flush work – bands of stone built into dark flint surrounds. Near here is Magdalen Street where over a decade ago the Civic Trust pioneered a cleaning-up operation. Since then a flyover for the new inner ring road has undone much of the good work, and the frontages are once again shabby and some depleted. A particularly sad loss has been the pioneer Calvert Street Methodist Church. There remain, however, the distinctive Old Meeting House, the Octagon Chapel, and the rebuilt St Mary's Baptist Church in this ancient area of nonconformity.

South of the river the Cathedral quarter shows much variety; outside the Cathedral, with the second highest Anglican Cathedral spire in England, and approached by two fine entrance gateways, is the grave of Nurse Edith Cavell, heroine of the First World War. The Cathedral's territory goes right down to the watergate on the Wensum. Though no longer in use it is known as Pull's Ferry; by this route came much of the Cathedral's building material.

The Cathedral has so many distinctive features of long standing that its recent improvements are not sufficiently understood. The Saxon bishop's throne is the only one north of the Alps, and may well have come from Thetford or North Elmham, seats of the diocese before it moved to Norwich. The cloisters are the largest among any at England's cathedrals and interesting for their evolving styles.

Not well known is the tremendous devotion of the Friends of the Cathedral, second in number only to those of Canterbury. Over the past 20 years the Cathedral's fabric has been made safe for many years ahead, and there have been outstanding developments towards making the Cathedral a social centre. Centre 71, a house in the Close where conferences and meetings not just Anglican but ecumenical are held, is only a stone's throw from the Cathedral shop carrying a very wide range of guides, local topographical books, pottery, pictures, metalwork and other *objets-d'art*. This now leads directly to a coffee bar over the cloisters where there is an assembly room for parties wishing to see over the Cathedral, or a special part of it not usually open such as the adjoining library, the treasury, or the cloisters with their splendid illuminated bosses.

Just across the road from the Cathedral is the mediaeval Augustine Steward's house tastefully transformed into the local office of the East Anglian Tourist Board chock-full of literature and tourist and traffic information for the whole of England's Eastern region. Also in the north-east quarter of Norwich is the Great Hospital, dating from 1249 and one of the oldest and most interesting almshouses in the country. Turning to the south-east quarter we encounter the old Musick House, the home of Jurnet the Jew, certainly Norwich's oldest dwelling (twelfth century). It has fine rooms of a later period upstairs to match the interesting cellars below. Moving through the centre of the city one cannot pass over the Castle Museum, one of the largest in the provinces, without noting the rotunda extension of recent years which has done so much to improve it as a social centre, complete with restaurant. The Theatre Royal has a more varied and continuous programme now than ever before; this, too, has been re-organised as a social centre providing meals and local exhibitions. The cloisters of St Andrew's Hall, the city's principal concert hall and a former Dominican Friary, have been converted into an exhibition centre.

We must not forget that the famous Maddermarket Theatre has recently been extended without detracting from its architectural charm. The Theatre Royal's next-door neighbour, the eighteenth-century Assembly House, was restored in 1950, and is a most popular venue for societies' meetings and one-man exhibitions. Just across the road is one of Britain's finest central libraries, including an archives centre. The spreading University in Denys Lasdun's Aztec style has grown up entirely in the past twelve years. It also offers many concerts, lectures and exhibitions to the Norwich public, and even a fully equipped bar.

It is impossible to survey Norwich's thirty-odd mediaeval churches, many of them over-the-water, but mention should be made of St Peter Mancroft, a fine Perpendicular church of splendid proportions wherein is buried the philosopher-physician Thomas Browne. Different in scale is the church of St Julian, commemorating the anchoress who was the first woman to write a book in English. To Norwich we must go for the country's largest Roman Catholic church not of cathedral rank,

St John's, a building of massive proportions in the Decorated style and with fine modern glass, the whole not yet a century old.

With so much to offer it is not surprising that Norwich produces one of Britain's finest provincial newspapers, the *Eastern Daily Press*. Turning to its 'what's on' feature is a much more rewarding experience than similar activity in many other county towns. Programmes ahead for two theatres, not to mention summer shows on the coast; fêtes, cinemas, gardens open at the week-end, flower festivals and (seasonably) numerous summer invitations to pick your own fruit. This paper, too, gives a clue to local industry – insurance, confectionery, food manufacture, chemicals, boots and shoes, light engineering, brewing and wine-making, printing, banking and construction.

Great Yarmouth, the second town in Norfolk, falls next for discussion. It is not so much in contrast to Norwich as one might suppose, for around the Quay are still numerous signs of its ancient history. The Fishermen's Hospital, the stalls of fried and fresh fish, the remnants of the narrow rows, keeping out cold winds, down which used to live numerous fishermen and prosperous merchants, give a clue to the town's former basic occupation, fishing. The Prunier trophy used to be awarded annually for the largest catch of fish, and it is less than 20 years since the annual October invasion of the Scots fisher girls intent on herring gutting ceased. It is to Great Yarmouth's credit that it has discovered other prosperities – food-freezing, power, oil from the North Sea and other light industry, not to mention tourism. Many who come for a week or a fortnight to Great Yarmouth never realise it is a town with a long history, with two surviving merchants' houses of great distinction and charm in use as museums, and a further museum on a ship, the *Lydia Eva*, a surviving steam boat. There is also the Tolhouse, thirteenth-century centre of the town's government, adjoining the newly-built Public Library, now, along with its Art Gallery, a true community centre.

Although the holiday-maker perambulating the Golden Mile (and there are four miles of front at Yarmouth) recks not of it, the key to the history of the resort, which dates only from the setting up of a bath house in 1759, can be discovered in the three piers. The oldest, the Jetty, where Nelson used to land on his way to see Lady Hamilton at the old Star Inn, was built in 1566, purely as a utility. By 1927, after several re-buildings, its shelters were glassed over. The Wellington Pier was built in 1853 and the Britannia Pier in 1857.

Yarmouth has certainly done its best to match up to Brighton in the south and Blackpool in the north-west as a resort, though it has perhaps not quite succeeded despite miles of sands, a huge caravan site on the Denes, small lakes, sports grounds, model village, shrubberies and at the end a large pleasure fair. In Great Yarmouth one can attend horse races, play golf, fly around the town, or shop in the most modern emporia. Even the blitzed Parish Church strikes a modern note for it has been restored in a manner which emphasises its huge area, and with splendid richly-glowing modern glass narrating the town's connection with the sea. Yet presiding over all is the lofty tower commemorating Nelson, topped by Britannia, back to the sea, glancing across to the South Quay to indicate where Yarmouth's power and prestige once exclusively lay.

King's Lynn is unquestionably the third of Norfolk's towns, with a far-reaching history. Never has such attention been paid to its charms as now. For 25 years it has housed an annual festival of music and the arts which is invariably patronised by the Queen Mother. A walled town, like Great Yarmouth and Norwich, it differed from them in being under episcopal control for some centuries as Bishop's Lynn, until Henry VIII took it over in 1537. During the Civil War in the next century Lynn sided with the King when nearly all Norfolk supported Cromwell.

Like the two larger towns, Lynn boasts of a magnificent church quite exceptionally bearing two western towers. It has a mediaeval lectern and two huge brasses, one illustrating the peacock feast Robert Braunche gave as Mayor of Lynn for Edward III (1349). Noteworthy is the extensive pedestrianisation of large shopping areas which has unfortunately led to the demolition of several fine old houses, notably the alleged home of George Vancouver, the voyager. By contrast the old mediaeval Hanseatic warehouses, where ships of the famous Northern League used to lay up their stores, Thoresby College, a former religious house, and Hampton Court have been splendidly restored as modern habitations. Like Norwich, Lynn was highly acclaimed in European Architectural Heritage Year.

Having commented on Norfolk's three largest towns, we are in a quandary as to what to cover next among much richness. Agriculture is, of course, the staple industry of the county; townsman and countryman meet each summer at the most successful Royal Norfolk Show, which serves to introduce the latest equipment as well as to appraise the finest cattle. However, this is no place to speak of Turnip Townshend, or the sheep shearings of Coke of Norfolk, or the supersession of steam threshing by the hired tractor. Norfolk is of great interest to geologists and gives proof that the Rhine once extended as far west as Cromer at a time when England was still joined to the continent of Europe.

Broadland and Breckland are quite unique and something must be said of them. The Broads are a series of lakes mostly in Norfolk but partly in Suffolk though quite unlike those of the Lake district or of central Scotland. In the first case they are man made; in the second they provide no superb mountain vistas for pedestrians or motorists who reach their shores. Pleasure lies almost exclusively with those who sail on them. As G. Christopher Davies has written: 'In a journey through (Broadland) by rail, you see nothing but its flatness; walk along its roads, you see the dullest side of it; but take to its water-highways, and the glamour of it steals over you.' Originally the main interest of the Broads was to the wildfowler or reed-cutter but following the works of G. Christopher Davies in the later years of the nineteenth century the pleasures of sailing became increasingly popular. In those days sail was the sole motive power and adventurers would not set forth without a deckhand to prepare their meals and undertake the laborious tasks of berthing or fetching fresh water – though the early books on the Broads suggest their waters are drinkable!

Now all is changed. In the summer season various capacious craft, including some capable of making the cross channel journey to Holland or Belgium, crowd the waters, especially the popular Wroxham and Salhouse Broads. What shall the speed limit be? What price the mooring charges? Where to deposit litter or sewage? – these are the problems continually argued between the boat-owners' association, the river authorities and Norfolk naturalists, for the larger speedier craft scour the banks destroying the haunts of birds and animals, their passengers bringing bustle and noise to the quiet seclusion of the waterside.

To the south-west of Broadland is Breckland, the waste heathland unsuitable for agricultural pursuits but the home of numerous rare birds, and the former home of neolithic man. Much of this area is now given over to the pine forests of the Forestry Commission.

North-west are the Fens and Marshland, the former with rich black soil and the dullest of landscape stretching for many miles without even a hedge. The Marshland is the home of marvellous churches, particularly at Terrington St Clement's, Tilney All Saints' and West Walpole. We can forgive the region's unending sameness for the marvellous crops of soft fruit and flowers its black soil produces. Unfortunately the stylish capital of the Fens, Wisbech, is just 15 miles outside our county.

'The whole of Norfolk is a treasure haven for the geologist, archaeologist, naturalist, architect, historian and artist, but probably no one part has greater appeal than the north-coast', wrote Andrew Stephenson. West of Lynn the coast is all made-up land. Westernmost Hunstanton tries to vie with easternmost Great Yarmouth, but it is only a century old and at first, after the royal family came to Sandringham, tried to build up an exclusive reputation. It was the advent of the railway which endeared it to the masses from the Midlands. Just south of Hunstanton is Snettisham, where was quarried carstone for hundreds of homes and other buildings with the West Norfolk look – lines of gingerbread slices perhaps intercalated with brick, flint or imported grey stone. Some of the finest examples of carstone are on the royal estate south of Hunstanton.

Further around, Brancaster, Wells, Morston, Blakeney, Cley and Salthouse are the home of sailing and ornithology. Nowhere else in Britain is there anything quite like this stretch of coast where one's disappointment at seeing the sea so far away changes to delight on discovering innumerable creeks and footpaths leading towards it. Sheringham, Cromer, Mundesley, Great Yarmouth and Gorleston complete the circle of the Norfolk coast with traditional beaches. Cromer and Sheringham, like Hunstanton, boast of cliffs, and this part of the coast is delightfully wooded.

No introductory survey of Norfolk can fail to mention its country churches, of which 659 built before AD 1700 survive. 'Some are miracles of soaring lightness with wooden angels in their high-up roofs: some have painted screens, or Georgian box pews, or mediaeval carved bench ends or ancient stained glass. Each is different from its neighbour, even if it is less than a mile off or in the same churchyard. None is without a treasure of some sort in wood, stone, iron, tile or glass. Some are famous throughout Britain' (Sir John Betjeman). Norfolk has, in fact, more surviving mediaeval churches than any other county. Considering that all the stone used in Norfolk churches for mouldings, arches and piers had to be brought in from other counties, possibly from Northamptonshire, and in some cases from abroad, this is a staggering total. The principal characteristic of Norfolk churches is often the round tower – an economical form of construction where small flints provided ready-to-hand building materials in the absence of building stone.

The fittings in Norfolk churches are so numerous and of such splendour that if they were dismantled the county's museum resources would be quite unable to place them. Only Somerset can rival Norfolk in the quantity and quality of its painted screens. Fortunately the county has a very strong body of Friends who are doing all they can to try to ensure that not one Norfolk church is destroyed, though all may not be used for religious purposes. Much publicity to the cause of Norfolk churches has been given by the Poet Laureate, Sir John Betjeman, and the proposed new edition of Munro Cautley's *Norfolk Churches* (1949) will give an added fillip to the forces of restoration. Akin to the churches, the many monastic and other ecclesiastical remains give visitors much enjoyment.

Norfolk's rivers are mainly used for pleasure rather than trade, but grain is still delivered up the Yare to Read's mill, just before Foundry Bridge, Norwich. Up to a decade ago the local evening paper recorded the weekly shipments of 'Norwich a port'. The Yare, the Bure and the Waveney (often the boundary with Suffolk) are the most attractive Norfolk rivers, but the Great Ouse draining into King's Lynn is undoubtedly the most commercially important stream; it contributed to placing Lynn among the most noted British ports in the early nineteenth century.

As remarkable and varied as Norfolk's churches are its country houses, thick on the ground because of the region's high importance in the national economy until the late eighteenth century. Few counties can rival Norfolk in its muster of stately homes – Holkham, Houghton, Blickling, Oxburgh, Felbrigg, Raynham, Wolterton, Euston, are only the most famous. Even more remarkable are those lesser homes, opened if at all only to private parties. East Barsham manor, Middleton Tower, Horsham St Faith with its recently discovered wall paintings are typical of the scores of smaller homes. Even where a house is not open to the public its garden very often is, though perhaps only on Gardeners' Sunday, normally in the Spring. Each Saturday's *Eastern Daily Press* lists several houses or gardens to be opened on the following day – not only the regulars such as Blickling, whose garden matches up to the hall it adjoins, but groups of cottage gardens at Hingham, perhaps; or Talbot Manor, which may not be so delightful as Anglesea Abbey or Sandringham or Stody Lodge, but which contains the largest collection of orchids in Britain. If you think only of garden produce you are well situated in Norfolk where during the quite lengthy fruit-growing season the ubiquitous *Eastern Daily Press* will list numerous 'pick your own' invitations; strawberries at 10p and blackberries 12p per pound in 1975. Even with the present price of petrol these invitations are well followed up by housewives anxious to fill their deep-freezers for the winter. Small wonder of the opportunities for amateurs when every 12 pounds of black-currants plucked attracts only 44p from the growers. Another recent heavy use for garden produce is for church flower festivals – and Norfolk provides two or three such events most weekends from spring to autumn.

We have listed the regions of our county and given some detail about Norwich, Great Yarmouth and King's Lynn though we have not been so bold as to discuss individually the next range of places. (Some are covered in the notes to the illustrations which follow.) We refer to Thetford, Watton, Cromer, Diss, Holt, Downham Market, East

Dereham, New Buckenham, Hunstanton, North Walsham, Reepham, Sheringham, Swaffham, Fakenham, Wells and Wymondham all of which would scorn to be regarded as villages.

Before looking finally at the contributions of other writers faced with a similar task to ours, we will mention one final interest – railways. As if to compensate for the wholesale removal of branch railway lines from Norfolk in the past 15 years there are no fewer than three regular operatives in the north, centre and south of Norfolk. The North Norfolk Railway, operating from Sheringham station to Weybourne on summer Saturdays has accumulated a considerable amount of rolling stock and two former L.N.E.R. steam locomotives, though none are from the parent Midland and Great Northern Railway. It plans to extend its route beyond Weybourne to Kelling Heath. At Barton House, Wroxham, the realistic though miniature Barton House Railway runs once a month in summer in aid of local charities. Among its appurtenances are a full-sized signal box. Finally, Mr Alan Bloom demonstrates an even larger model railway and several full-sized express locomotives at his splendid gardens at Bressingham near Diss.

The dominance of Norwich apart there can be little coherence or unity in any description of the county. Breckland, apart from the Stanford battle area is mainly afforested. Poppyland around Cromer and Sheringham, has gone for good, sacrificed to modern efficient farming, like numerous Norfolk hedgerows. 'In my garden of sleep where the poppies are bred, I wait for the living alone with the dead', wrote Clement Scott. His cult hereabouts survived the First World War, with the popularity of the Flanders poppy as a sentimental emblem. Is Cromer still the gem of the Norfolk coast now that with the decline of the railway and the competition of foreign package tours the Edwardian month-long family sojourns are at an end? When under the recent local government re-organisation North Norfolk had the opportunity of taking the name Pastonacres to strengthen its traditions it would have none of it, perhaps because the North Sea oil terminal counts for more in those parts now than the long-forgotten famous letter-writing family. However, Broadland, though changed by the encroachment of power on sail, is as popular as ever.

We will conclude this survey with three seventeenth-century comments and one from our own century on Norfolk. Thomas Fuller said that 'all England may be carved out of Norfolk, represented therein, not only to the kind, but degree thereof. Here are fens and heaths, and light and deep, and sand and clay ground, and meadow and pasture and arable, and woody and (generally) woodless land . . . . Norfolk collectively taken hath a sufficient result of pleasure and profit, that being supplied in one part which is defective in another.'

Henry Gurney, writing somewhat earlier on Norfolk said:

Soyle it hath, land, pasture, meade and woode
the heath and ffenn, the marish, lake and meare
to beastes and fowle a shelture and a foode
wherby yt doth so great a plenty beare
one half the sea the rest sweet streames surrounde
and so with fish no less it doth abounde.

The anonymous author of *The Chorography of Norfolk* (probably written about 1617 by John Norden) considered Norfolk to be 'a populous and fruitful county mostly open and playne, very rich and stored in itself of all things necessary for the sustenance of man's life. Corn it beareth very good in great plenty in most parts of the shire. . . . It is well stored with conies and sheep and food for them both good and sufficient. It is well watered with rivers and brooks and well stored with wood and fuell. For fishing, fowling hunting and hawking and all gentle manly sports and exercises it is behind no shire in the land.'

'What should I write more of it, the goodness, fruitfulness and pleasantries of it may be esteemed by the complexion and subtiltie of the inhabitants. . . . Norfolk wyles many a man beguiles.'

R. H. Mottram, most celebrated of recent writers on Norfolk generally, said: 'Norfolk offers everything that . . . seekers after relaxation and recreation are looking for. It is the second largest county in England, containing infinite variety. . . . Although not so thoroughly "discovered" as many coastal counties, Norfolk is well worth a visit. After all the King (1950) lives there; was born there. Isn't that good enough?'

KING'S LYNN: THE CUSTOM HOUSE

King's Lynn is best entered by the South gate, in the shadow of which is the Honest Lawyer inn bearing a sign of the lawyer with his head tucked underneath his arm.

Lynn is recorded in Domesday Book and in AD 1100, some ten years later, was placed under episcopal rule by Bishop Herbert de Losinga. William de Turbe, the next bishop but one, extended its endowments to take in the Tuesday market and the chapel of St Nicholas so that it became known as Bishop's Lynn until 1537 when Henry VIII confiscated the bishop's lands and changed the town's name to King's Lynn.

In the Middle Ages King's Lynn became a great port, being the natural gateway to the continent for the nearby river traffic. Warehouses and stately homes remain as a legacy of this period; also two notable communal housing sites, Hampton Court and Thoresby College, now restored and occupied.

The graceful Custom House was built in 1683 by Henry Bell, a former Mayor of Lynn. None of its sides is equal to any of the rest, as many an architectural drawing student has discovered when asked to make a scale drawing of the building. At one time the arched lower floor was open to merchandise.

The King's Lynn Festival has annually brought to the town numerous visitors for over 25 years, as interested in the environment as in the programme. Bell's Custom House fits very appropriately into the festival setting.

14 C. WINLOVE 14

HAPPISBURGH LIGHTHOUSE

This view of Happisburgh epitomises what is most sought after in rural Norfolk by those seeking an old-fashioned holiday – a quiet village close to the sea producing corn – though in today's agricultural efficiency lacking the colour of Poppyland (the name given by the poet Clement Scott at the turn of the century to the scarlet summer fields to the north). Yet time has not stood still at Happisburgh; there is a modern unobtrusive caravan site, a new 300 ft high Norfolk signalling mast, and a new in-shore lifeboat.

The tower of Happisburgh church is one of the finest vantage points in Norfolk. The church raised enough funds for an extensive restoration between the wars and to re-hang the bells, and later repaired the damage done by the Nazis bombs. Some Germans were indeed temporarily buried in the churchyard, but the biggest mass grave, north of the church, contains 119 officers and men from the *Invincible* lost off Happisburgh in August 1802, like myriads of other vessels. Happisburgh's windmill has disappeared.

Happisburgh lighthouse has no rival for interest in Norfolk. In 1791 two lighthouses were built, one near the sea being 70 feet high, and the present higher one 84 feet. Changes of fuel, and improvement in lenses had made so much progress by 1883 that the lower light was dismantled. Tourists will never reach this sequestered spot, even guided by the prominent red bands of the lighthouse, if they ask for Happisburgh. The appropriate local reply is 'I know it oughter be Happisburgh, but its such a mouthful that Hazebro's good enough for me'.

OXBURGH HALL

Oxburgh Hall is a shining example of what the National Trust can do by splendid housekeeping. It is one of the finest moated houses in Britain, even though it lacks a lengthy series of state rooms. Built about 1482 the Hall was attacked and damaged by the Parliamentarians towards the end of the Civil War (1647). Its interior was completely re-arranged in the early nineteenth century and though outwardly homogeneous, presents an interesting variety of styles. 'The moat can hardly have contributed more to defence against concerted attack than the Hall itself, built at a time when fortified castles were already out of date. While adding to the scenic beauty of Oxburgh it supplied little more than a slight deterrent to co-ordinated attack.' (A. L. Bedingfeld.) The elder Pugin declared that the gatehouse is 'one of the noblest specimens of domestic architecture of the fifteenth century which . . . remains in a perfect state'. Equalled by Layer Marney, Essex, it has no rivals in Norfolk. Its most interesting feature is a newel brick staircase astonishingly accurately built with a moulded brick handrail, the barrel vault forming one continuous spiral.

Inside the main house is the King's room, so called because Henry VII lodged in it in 1487. It now contains the bed on which are displayed hangings partly worked by Mary Queen of Scots and Bess of Hardwick, the Countess of Shrewsbury. Visitors should also see the Roman Catholic chapel, the ruined parish church and the adjoining terracotta tombs in the Bedingfeld chantry.

NORWICH: TOMBLAND ALLEY

The greensward adjoining the pathway of Tombland alley is the churchyard of St George's Tombland, though the graves are unrelated to the name. The view is typical of so much of central Norwich where refurbished and restored ancient houses jostle together with the odd inserted humble modern structure. The central opening is under the house of Augustine Steward, thrice mayor of Norwich, who thoroughly deserves his memorial. In 1534 the Guildhall, the centre of the City's administration until 1938, was in bad repair though only just over a hundred years old. Steward launched an appeal and supervised the repairs which took two years and cost £208.50! Built about 1530, Steward's house was never put to better use than at the present time as the Norwich centre of the East Anglian Tourist Board; here in the charming timber-fronted rooms visitors may obtain a wide range of guide books, lists of hotels and lodgings, maps and souvenirs. Furthermore, Steward's house faces across Tombland to the main entrance to the Cathedral, which also has an attractive shop along similar lines, the co-existence of the two (and another good retailer's higher up Tombland) proving yet again that competition more often stimulates than destroys.

Tombland? It has nothing to do with tombs but means vacant land. In fact it was the centre of Norwich for some centuries until the Normans established the present Market Square as the centre.

BLAKENEY

Westwards from Sheringham, Norfolk suffers a sea change and we reach a series of ports of long ago, hidden now behind numerous creeks and saltmarshes. Best known of these is Blakeney, where those who enjoy paddling, sailing, picking samphire or sea-lavender or just sitting in the car reading their newspapers can all be accommodated.

The Quay at Blakeney presents many surprises. According to the time of tide there are youngsters scrambling over the brown and yellow beach, accompanied by their dogs, or sailing safely in the deepening channel. To the stranger's astonishment there is no view of the sea. For that he must journey to Blakeney point where, in Spring, one must take care not to step on seabirds' eggs. It is well worth taking binoculars to distinguish uncommon birds or the seals quietly basking on the sand banks just off shore.

Blakeney village originally comprised little more than one steep row of cottages down to the quay and the modern hotel shown. Near here too is the supposed Guildhall, a stone-built undercroft with brick vaulting. Blakeney's attraction lies in the care with which its inhabitants look after its flint cottages and their gardens.

Immediately behind the village on a lofty site stands the king-sized church with its prominent so-called beacon tower, additional to the 100-ft high West tower.

BLICKING HALL

Few country houses can present passers-by with such a surprise as can Jacobean Blickling. The towers and Dutch gables are straightforward enough, but the pinnacles and cupola beckon one to approach between two amazingly long ranges of yew flanking the approach road.

Controversy still rages as to whether Anne Boleyn, best known of Henry VIII's queens, ever lived at Blickling. Her ancestor Geoffrey Boleyn certainly owned it at one time, though before the present house was built. Its creator was Robert Lyminge, who had previously had so much to do with the building of Hatfield House. Work at Blickling began between 1616–25, five years after Hatfield was completed.

Much of Blickling dates back only to the eighteenth century, when Thomas Ivory of Norwich made several changes, including the filling of the original great hall to form an entrance hall with a double stairway. An effigy of Anne Boleyn is here. The original long gallery now acts as a library; the plaster ceiling is most impressive. Most colourful is the room with the tapestry showing Peter the Great of Russia. This was presented to the 2nd earl of Buckinghamshire, who lived at Blickling, by Catherine the Great to mark his term as ambassador. The gardens, laid out with a formality becoming unfashionable, caused Hannah More to say that 'the park, wood and water of this place are superior to those on any of the neighbouring estates'.

BUXTON MILL

Although they do not assume such a prominent place on the skyline, Norfolk watermills have, on the whole, lasted longer than its windmills. Visitors do not go to them purely for their architectural qualities; mostly they are constructed of brick and weatherboarding. They find little or no place in the usual guide books to the county. Fortunately, a few years ago Miss Philippa Miller, 'possessing the unusual combination of talent, perception and modesty' brought out a much needed book on Norfolk watermills, some of which date back at least to Domesday Book (1086). The decline of watermills has been continuous since the middle ages, and is due to the growth of windmills, the Black Death, the dissolution of the monasteries, fires, floods, and the introduction of steam power in the late eighteenth century. The great Norwich flood of 1912, and economic factors stemming from the two great wars of our time, have similarly cut down the number of watermills in Norfolk, of which any trace can be found, to 56. In 1968 only 18 of them were working.

Buxton Mill was working from at least 1754 until a few years ago, but has now been converted to tea rooms and a craft centre with rooms devoted to painting, modelling and second-hand books. Teas are served and the mill is fast developing a reputation as an arts centre with numerous widely-advertised exhibitions. The photograph shows the main front, but the rear view, including the Bure mill-pool, is almost equally exciting and it looks as though the building's future is now quite secure.

CASTLE RISING

Castle Rising is trebly blest. There is the castle, the famous bedehouse whose lady residents turn out in their scarlet cloaks on state occasions, and the equally fine parish church with some of the finest Norman work in Britain. The bedehouse, Trinity Hospital, dates from 1609–11. From 1558–1832 30 or 40 parliamentary electors returned two members. The votes were controlled by the Howard family, catholic then as today, and perhaps the most famous man who acquired a seat because of their influence was Samuel Pepys, the diarist. Sir Robert Walpole, the first British prime minister, also represented Castle Rising for some time.

Rising was a seaport town when Lynn was but a marsh
Now Lynn it is a seaport town and Rising fares the worse.

St Felix, who converted to Christianity many in the district of Norfolk where Lynn lies, is believed to have landed at Castle Rising about 630 AD.

Much excavation has been carried out recently around the stone keep of Castle Rising, and a chapel and some associated domestic buildings have been unearthed. The pottery discovered does not come from as far afield as might have been expected in view of Rising's former status as a port. However the excavations, part of which are shown in the picture, have added to the interest of a visit to the keep, and there is no better way of spending a fine Norfolk day than to visit Castle Rising.

NORWICH CATHEDRAL

It is impossible to do justice to Norwich Cathedral in a short space: we can only point to certain outstanding features. The Cathedral is approached by one of two gates to the upper close. The Ethelbert gate has fine flushwork, flint mixed with stone, and a series of canopied niches. Even more striking is the Erpingham gate, a hundred yards or so down Tombland, the name of the street from which the Cathedral is approached. It has a wide arch in a flint gable and a statue of the builder, Sir Thomas Erpingham, together with other figures and heraldic devices. Facing this gate is the Cathedral's West front, regarded as its worst feature, but on the left are some interesting old buildings belonging to the Norwich school which is still within the Cathedral precinct.

The picture from the south-west shows the immense nave, the South transept, several of the houses in the pleasant close (now reasonably free of cars), and the loftiest cathedral spire in England (315 ft.) save only Salisbury. Inside the Cathedral, the fine Norman nave, the cloisters, the largest in any cathedral, and the Saxon bishop's throne, believed to have been brought from Elmham where the Cathedral was sited before it moved to Norwich, are the outstanding features plus the magnificent series of illuminated bosses. In the past 25 years, tremendous efforts have been made to put the Cathedral in full repair and a treasury, a shop, a coffee bar and an exhibition centre have been created. A pleasant walk has been opened up from the Cathedral to its water gate on the river.

NORWICH: ELM HILL

Andrew Stephenson's edition of Arthur Mee's *Norfolk* describes Elm Hill as 'the most visited and the most photographed street in Norwich'. Its charm consists in its homogeneity, but it was only as comparatively recently as 1927 that it was saved from destruction when many of its houses were derelict. The individual buildings are not in themselves outstanding, with the exception of the Strangers' Hall, well down on the left, but several have had interesting histories. Moreover Norwich Corporation has paid great attention to the street furniture, and in 1975 Elm Hill took first place in a competition for street lighting organised by the International Commission on Illumination. Tudor, Stuart and Georgian fronts all blend, pleasantly colour-washed, and the cobbles add to the appearance and deter the occasional car. It is, unfortunately, not possible to approach each building from the rear.

The Briton's Arms on the right of the picture by the elm tree is probably the oldest house in Elm Hill, the only one to have escaped a disastrous fire in 1507. A coffee house, it has at different times sheltered worsted weavers, leather workers and shoemakers.

Elm Hill has been a street of merchants' houses and a slum, and is now a fine specialised area where personal attention is given in the shops. Antiques, pictures, fine clothing and stamps are some of the interests covered. 'There is not a single house in Elm Hill which could be disturbing', concluded Sir Nikolaus Pevsner.

THE MONASTERY

GREAT YARMOUTH: THE FISHERMEN'S HOSPITAL

Widely famed with its neighbour Gorleston-on-Sea as 'the resorts that have everything', Great Yarmouth has done much to care for what historic features it has retained following severe war damage. There is little resemblance between the Golden Mile, one of Britain's finest sea-side promenades, with every kind of gift shop, a fun fair and pleasant gardens, and the old port.

Most of what is interesting abuts on the large Market Square, or its extension Church Plain, notably St Nicholas' church rebuilt in a bright, modern idiom without discarding the Gothic shell of the old church. Part of the extensive town walls are here. To reach the quays and the river it was formerly possible to go through 145 rows – narrow passages between houses cramming *multum in parvo* because of Yarmouth's restricted site. Most were lost in the blitz which destroyed the church.

The Fishermen's Hospital is centrally situated between the beach resort and the historic quays, adding dignity to its surroundings. Founded in 1702 for 20 fishermen and their wives, it is neatly built and paved. The central statue represents Charity, and the cupola contains a figure of St Peter.

Hospital
For Decayed Fishermen
founded by
The Corporation
1702

CROMER

How far does Cromer deserve its title of 'gem of the Norfolk coast'? Only marginally larger than Sheringham it does add an ancient history to the other claims to recognition that its old rival brings forward. By AD 1400 the town of Shipden annexed to Crowmere had been washed into the sea, but not before the inhabitants had realised that their church was fated and had started building another church on the present site.

It was not until Victorian wealth and the railway reached Cromer that the present fine church came to dominate the whole town. The church was thoroughly restored to its present state in 1887–9.

With the decline in long residential holidays, the householders who would cater for Edwardian and Georgian families gave way to more flexible hoteliers. Now some of these are finding life difficult. A few hotels have been demolished. The old attraction of Poppyland, to the East of Cromer, no longer exists; the First World War's sentimental attachment to the striking red blossom has been overtaken by a finer husbandry where poppies among the corn spell inefficiency.

The lifeboat service, and particularly the exploits of the legendary Henry Blogg, coxswain 1909–47, carry on the traditions of the old fishing village. This has practically disappeared, but many old houses adapted to shops still stand to diversify this intimate resort which continues to maintain its pier and concert party. Interestingly the lifeboat station and launching slope are at the pier's end.

WYMONDHAM: THE MARKET CROSS

An attractive dormitory area for Norwich, Wymondham now houses 10,000 inhabitants. At the centre in the High Street stands the Market Cross. It dates from 1617, when a great fire destroyed over 300 houses and the old cross. Its open area for the bulkier merchandise is bounded by eight posts, and there is an upper storey and exterior staircase. There are arched bracings and a central post with steps around where vendors could shelter from the elements. Early this century the market cross was a library and reading room.

Among streets of unspoiled seventeenth- and eighteenth-century buildings we must mention the half-timbered Green Dragon inn with its projecting eaves, and Becket's chapel, rebuilt about 1400 as a chantry chapel. It is now the Wymondham branch of the Norfolk County Library since the Market Cross gave up that role.

Chapel and inn are near the pine-fringed walk to the Abbey church which surprises us in having two lofty towers, legacy of ancient feuds between monks and populace, each building their own. The interior, gleaming with a golden reredos and canopy, matches the outside.

From Wymondham, after the Reformation, Robert Kett led a rebellion to combat landowners who were enclosing common and church lands. His army of 16,000 was finally overwhelmed, he being hanged in Norwich, and his brother William from Wymondham church tower.

BUS
STOP
STATION
ASTMANS

HEYDON

Weavers' Green of the short-lived television serial, Heydon's fame as one of England's most charming villages is due in large measure to its being on the road to nowhere, except the Lord of the Manor's seat. Heydon Hall was built in 1581–4 and is crowned with a picturesque nest of chimneys. Two members of the Bulwer family achieved national fame in the nineteenth century; Henry Lord Dalling (1801–72) who filled ambassadorial posts at Madrid and Washington, and Edward Lord Lytton (1803–73), the novelist.

The charm of Heydon village lies not so much in any one feature, but in the sum of its parts. The capacious green holds a Gothick brick canopy over the village pump, and the village street is completely unspoiled. Heydon follows the practice of many Norfolk villages in regularly opening up some of its gardens; like those of Hingham, their charm stems not from their size but from their intimate style. One has a lake, a cricket field and a pigeon loft.

The church has several points of distinction, including a fifteenth-century pulpit and the huge tomb of a former Norwich M.P., Erasmus Earle, under a slab twelve feet by six feet. This tomb is supposed to have damaged three bridges on its way here, and to have broken the back of one of the men who set it in position.

SANDRINGHAM

With its interior opened to the public for the first time shortly, Sandringham House, the Queen's Norfolk residence whose gardens are already a great delight, will be a very popular venue for Norfolk tourists. The house, designed by A. J. Humbert, dates only from 1870 except for a conservatory from the former demolished house designed by S. S. Teulon, a High Gothic Victorian architect. The East-front picture shows the main entrance and the window of the room where the Duke of Clarence died in 1892, which bears a plaque. The ballroom on the left was added in 1883 by a third architect, R. W. Edis. On the far right is the private garden developed by George VI so that he could walk to the main gates unobserved.

Edward VII, who probably spent more time at Sandringham than any succeeding monarch, would have preferred Newstead Abbey near Nottingham, but negotiations fell through. His mother, Queen Victoria, was glad her son was not going to live among associations of the wicked poet Byron, but she never cared for Sandringham, and only visited the house twice.

Sandringham will certainly not present as many treasures as other Norfolk houses, but it will be interesting to check whether the personalities of its main châtelaines still show – Queen Alexandra's fussiness and love of clutter, or Queen Mary's precision and delight in embroidery.

To visit the former village church in Sandringham park is a unique experience for it is embellished with a solid silver altar and a silver-encased pulpit, given by Rodman Wanamaker, a great admirer of Edward VII. Here, too, are many portrait plaques of great interest.

CLEY MILL

Cley is less well-known than Blakeney or Wells, possibly because its beach is only attained over a steep bank of shingle beyond which the North Sea seems particularly menacing. It is one of the gradually lessening number of attractive East Anglian coastal townships not yet bypassed by the coastal road where every house has individual distinction in its variety of flint or warm brick. The windmill is one of the few remaining Norfolk mills bearing sails. It is a tower mill where the top cap and fantail are driven around by the sails. This type of mill was fairly common in Norfolk, used either for draining the marshland or grinding corn.

The marshlands at Cley are protected by the National Trust and are a favourite haunt of bird-watchers.

Like its neighbours, Cley was a flourishing port until the eighteenth century, with a fine harbour and a clear access by creek to the sea. Land reclamation in the eighteenth century destroyed the harbour.

The church was rebuilt in the fourteenth century with a much larger population in view than the 500 who now live here. The unusual clerestory, with large wheel windows alternating with pointed ones, indicates the scale of the building but the south transept early fell into ruin (or perhaps, on account of the Black Death, was never completed).

CASTLE ACRE

The castle mound at Castle Acre demands attention before the priory: William the Conqueror granted the castle to his son-in-law, William de Warenne. Its limits are marked by the thirteenth-century gateway at the end of the present main street, although no other early Norman architecture survives. More information on the huge grass mound is awaited from recent excavations which have revealed a number of walls long buried.

West of the castle and nearer the river Nar the West front of the Cluniac priory equals in grandeur the spectacular remains of Byland and the other famous Yorkshire abbeys. One of the first religious houses of its order to be founded in England, it promised a more attractive form of service than the Benedictine in the opinion of its founder William de Warenne, son of the founder of the castle. The priory was inhabited long after the Dissolution and there is an interesting model of it in its heyday in the Tudor guest house adjoining the West front, shown on the right of the picture. There are other extensive remains, well laid out by the Department of the Environment. A story is current about a tour of the priory by King George v and Queen Mary. Passing the garderobes the local guide was embarrassed at the King's enquiry as to their purpose and replied, 'Thas where they use'ta go, when they ha'ta go', at which the King laughed heartily.

The fine wide main street, running along Peddar's Way, a pre-Roman track, and the parish church are also of great interest.

RANWORTH BROAD

The lofty tower of the village church gives as good a Broads vantage point as any. Ranworth Staithe is a very popular halt for Broads voyagers. Less busy than Wroxham it also has more appeal, for here is an inn dressed out in nautical guise, a good landing stage, and a most interesting church, St Helen's, visited by 40,000 holiday-makers annually.

Six stalls in the chancel were probably taken from St Benet's abbey, just across the river, and the fifteenth-century screen is one of the finest in Norfolk. It is at present being restored in the confident hope that most of the black paint which was smeared over the features of saints therein depicted can be removed with modern restorative treatments.

In front of the screen stands a lectern with plainsong fastened to one side and so clearly intended for the choir leader. That singing played a big part in the worship of St Helen's is borne out by the presence in the church of an antiphoner (musical setting of the psalms), according to the Sarum use. The antiphoner at Ranworth is a folio manuscript of about the year 1400 written on sheepskin and lavishly illuminated. The pictures of Jonah with the whale are particularly fine.

Since it includes no motor craft our photograph records the true spirit of the Broads! There could be no finer sailing conditions than on Ranworth (or Malthouse) Broad.

GREAT MASSINGHAM

Norfolk is not a county of set-piece villages in the sense that Elm Hill could be regarded as a set-piece. Norfolk is so proud of its villages that it has more carved and painted village signs than any other county, and there is always tremendous enthusiasm annually for the best-kept village competition. Great Massingham is quite unselfconscious about these developments. It incorporates the remains of an Augustinian priory founded before AD 1260 in the buildings of the Abbey farm, and this was destroyed at the Reformation (1538).

The village's most striking features to those passing motorists who have chosen to drive through it to vary the scenery (it is on no main road) are its two ponds, thought by some to be the fish ponds of the defunct priory, but certainly so large, with appropriate green surroundings, that they seem the work of a professional landscape gardener.

The village once had a market and a fair, and with the neighbouring Little Massingham drew its importance from its proximity to the pre-Roman Peddar's way which slants its straight path diagonally across the north of the county. The village has its own pub in a part of the county where they are not very common.

Great Massingham's commanding church has a tall tower with a remarkably tall tower arch, a few fragments of old stained glass, and a good modern altar. The village has associations with Stephen Perse who founded the famous Perse school in Cambridge.

GREAT YARMOUTH: THE TOWN HALL AND RIVER YARE

The modern picture of the quay and municipal buildings fails to bring out what the town has lost in past years. The herring fishery dates at least from the thirteenth century. First the Dutch and later the Scots were the most successful of the nations trading to Yarmouth; the Scots 'brought their womenfolk with them to find employment in the gutting and curing sheds ashore. By 1900, Yarmouth had become the premier herring port in the world and in 1913 the eleven hundred and sixty three boats fishing out of the port caught 2,488,140 cwt. of fish. . . . Now no Scots fisher lasses are to be seen in Yarmouth and no drifters fish from the port' (Hedges).

Much more handsome than the present Town Hall were the Assembly rooms, on the same site. Classical in style, and with reasonable accommodation for up to the 400 gathered to wish prosperity to the mayor at Michaelmas-tide, they displayed a portico and two brass cannon taken by Nelson at Copenhagen.

Fortunately, though the fisher girls, the classical Assembly rooms, the trees and railway lines along the quay have gone with much else, trade involving the North Sea oil rigs, food freezing and light industry has made the port of Yarmouth as busy as ever it was, container ships plying to and from the Common Market countries. Inland the Yare is navigable as far as Norwich. And there are still several façades of merchants' former houses, visible in the picture, delightfully restored to the period of the quay's heyday.

Norwich Belle

HOVETON ST PETER CHURCH

Unfortunately for Hoveton most people who embark on the Broads or patronise the largest village stores in England believe themselves to be in Wroxham all the time. In fact, everything north of the river is in Hoveton. Ecclesiastically, Hoveton St John church is associated with the adjoining St Mary's church, Wroxham. Hoveton St Peter is now linked to Beeston St Lawrence and Ashmanaugh churches.

Hoveton St Peter is a small church with a charming thatched roof that illustrates the difficulties attendant upon the church authorities in Norfolk where there are 659 mediaeval churches, more than in any other county. St Peter's is not one of these, having been built in 1624, a very unusual time for building, though there had been an earlier church. The present sequestered church could be a school chapel, with its flower-lined approach and its concise dimensions; it measures 14 feet by 19.

The Norfolk Society recently published *Norfolk County Churches and the Future*, which dramatically highlights the problems of isolated churches which may now be declared redundant under a church pastoral measure of 1968. Will Hoveton St Peter ever be declared redundant, as it is less centrally sited than other larger and older churches? Time alone will tell.

COLTISHALL

There can be no greater contrast than the neighbouring river Bure villages of Wroxham and Coltishall. A summer Saturday at Wroxham has to be seen to be believed – vast crowds disembarking with their possessions and as many more ready to take over when the army of cleaners has removed the signs of someone else's holiday; others lacking the skill or energy to pilot their own boat stand ready to board *Princess Margaret*, *Her Majesty* or other covered-in launches holding upwards of 80 persons. Were we not talking about Saturday we could add boat-building to the sights.

Many of Coltishall's voyaging patrons move up-river through Belaugh to Coltishall to seek peace from just this Wroxham scene. Broadland memories are behind and quietness is acquired without having to sail up one of the Bure tributaries, for the river here is both broad and peaceful. Coltishall also attracts the motorist in search of quiet. The low river banks allow houses, the Rising Sun pub, and a spacious grassy field not marked private to approach quite close to the river; there can be few more attractive viewpoints of an animated river scene in Norfolk from an official car park.

Leaving the river aside, Coltishall, because of the age of many of its houses, is most attractive. The annual open days at R.A.F. Coltishall are unsurpassed for excitement and interest in all the latest developments in flying. The church of St John the Baptist has Anglo-Saxon work in its North wall.

BULLARDS' ALES

HOLKHAM HALL: THE ENTRANCE HALL

Approached closely, Holkham's exterior is somewhat pedestrian, and it is only if one looks back some distance on the longish walk to the column commemorating Coke of Norfolk (1752–1842) that the symmetry of the design, even to the matching chimney pots, can be appreciated.

The column commemorates Thomas Coke the agricultural reformer, not the builder of the house. This was an earlier Thomas Coke (1697–1759) who selected the Palladian style for his mansion on his return from Italy after a prolonged Grand Tour. The flight of red-carpeted stairs, the alabaster columns, golden frieze and classical statuary are quite breathtaking to visitors who can suspect nothing so grand from what they see outside. Here too is a coffered ceiling, and numerous classical statues and inlaid plaques.

The park, nine miles round, is as magnificent as the house. The tree planting of the first earl is commemorated by an inscription on the inside of the front door. 'This seat on an open barren estate was planned, planted, built, decorated and inhabitated in the middle of the eighteenth century by Thomas Coke, Earl of Leicester.'

Holkham is unique in adhering strictly to the classical models of William Kent and Matthew Brettingham, its architects, and in achieving such a quality in its furnishings that little has had to be changed in over two hundred years.

EAST BARSHAM:
THE MANOR AND GATE HOUSE

Less well known than it should be as it is only occasionally open to the public is East Barsham manor, which suddenly and unexpectedly greets travellers on the B1105 road from Fakenham. It was built of brick by Sir William Fermor during the reign of King Henry VIII (1509–47) and illustrates the fine contemporary decorative treatment of this material in contrast to its very plain use at Holkham, two centuries later.

There had been an earlier house on the site of the manor going back to the Conqueror, but the appearance of the present house owes much to the twentieth century through the agency of a succession of diligent owners. The gatehouse entrance is surmounted by Henry's royal arms and it and the house are crowned by brilliantly designed pinnacles. The ten chimneys, all of them different, are unequalled in splendour in Norfolk except at Little Snoring rectory, and the terracotta dressings add to the general appearance.

The house was originally moated and part of the moat is still traceable. Inside there is a 45 ft. long great hall with a minstrel's gallery. In 1974, when East Barsham primary school was searching for its own bell to celebrate an anniversary, the authorities turned up instead with a handsome bell from the Hall. As the house and the nearby church were ruinous well within the last century, few legends have grown up about them, but Henry VIII is reputed to have walked barefoot from here to the famous shrine at Walsingham in 1511 before the present house was built.